L For Lily

A play about brave men who fought
in the skies of 1943

by Steve Harper

SERVING THEATRE

SINCE 1830

WWW.SAMUELFRENCH.CO.UK
WWW.SAMUELFRENCH.COM

FOR AMATEUR
PRODUCTION ENQUIRIES

UNITED KINGDOM AND WORLD
EXCLUDING NORTH AMERICA
plays@SamuelFrench-London.co.uk
020 7255 4302/01

UNITED STATES AND CANADA
info@SamuelFrench.com
1-866-598-8449

Each title is subject to availability from Samuel French,
depending upon country of performance.

Glossary of abbreviations

Snook	Cheap and unpopular South African sea fish used in World War Two recipies. N.B. Unsold cans of fish at the end of the war were relabelled as cat food.
Opps Room	Operational Room where air battles were planned and monitored.
NAFFI	Navy, Army, Air Force Institution.
KCs	Kilo cycles (Hertz). The frequency of the carrier wave used for radio communication. Measured in thousands of cycles per second.
Happy Valley	The heavily defended Ruhr Valley.
M.O.	Medical Officer.
Fag	Cigarette.
180 on the nose	When the nose of the aircraft is in line with the runway.
Cookie	A large 1,000lb bomb.
ETA	Estimated Time of Arrival.
WAAF	Woman's Auxiliary Air Force.
Brylcreem boys	Slang term for male Air Force members.
W.O.	Warrant Officer.
Gong	Medal.
Gee	A radar system that worked by calculating the time delay between two radio signals.

Ground display	Radar that displayed ground contours.
Harmonic	Frequency that is a complex multiple of the original.
Flack	Shrapnel.
Feather Props	Alter the angle of the propellers to offer less wind resistance.
Salvo	Dropping bombs in succession.
Yolk	Aircraft steering column.

L for Lily was presented at the Princess Theatre, Hunstanton, on Friday, 10th July 2015. The cast was as follows:

Nose gunner	**ERIC**	TOM SAUNDERS
Captain	**SKIP**	RICHARD ABEL
Flight engineer	**NORMAN**	ROBERT HORNETT
Navigator	**ARTHUR**	WILLEM HARRISON BARRACLOUGH
Radio operator	**JOE**	STEVE HARPER
Mid upper gunner	**TAFF**	TOM TREE
Rear gunner	**TONY**	JEMIMA CUMMINGS

AUTHOR'S NOTE

In 1983 I worked for British Telecom as one of their cable testers. My job was to measure the parameters of copper cable either constructed by our own staff or purchased from one of the contract firms that supplied us. I had studied electrical transmission at college for five years and was considered one of the leading authorities – it was repetitive, methodical and lucrative work. But suddenly in 1983 everything changed. All my years of accumulating knowledge on sending signals with electricity became obsolete, the world of fibre optics and digital transmission had arrived when BT installed the first fibre optic cable from Barrington into Cambridge.

Apart from the staff at our research centre-fibre optic transmission was a black art, understood by very few and practised by fewer. I became a national expert very quickly. This is not a boast you understand, but more a confession. I knew very little, but that was more than everybody else, and in the kingdom of the blind, the one-eyed man is truly king!

I had written technical publications before so it was no great surprise when my boss decided that I should be the one to write a report on the new technology. Writing technical stuff is like being a member of a small exclusive club, you can use phrases like Iterative Impedance, resistivity and shot noise with confidence. Your audience is small, but they tend to be appreciative.

I am now retired, and on reflection there have been only a few life-changing moments in my existence, this however was one of them. A total accident really based on my line manager's sense of humour! I accepted my brief to explain the complexities of light transmission for our "In-house" magazine, and was packing up to get back to my own office when my manager, bless him, added one last caveat. I want, he said, a report that your wife would read, enjoy and understand. Aghhhhhhh.

I love my wife more then I could ever explain, but writing a technical report for somebody who doesn't know an ohm from a megahertz...tricky!

Well I did it. And surprisingly I enjoyed it. Lots of phrases such as, "You think a Usain Bolt is fast; but that's just peanuts compared to lasers turning on and off five hundred million times a second". Yes, OK, it's not big, and it's not clever, but it was my first bit of freestyle writing, and it was a success, and I loved it, and my wife read it. OK, there's nothing that wonderful woman wouldn't do for me.

A few years later I retired, and joined an amateur dramatics society. In 2005 they held a competition to write a pantomime. I wrote *The Curse of Coconut Island*, a pirate extravaganza. It won because nobody else submitted an entry. It had three acts and twenty seven scenes. I got better.

L for Lily came about because of my dad. He joined the RAF In 1939 and was the navigator on many bombing missions. It occurred to me that at 19 years old his life would have been like most young men's, but with the horror of war to contend with. Living in a small Norfolk town by day, but climbing into a petrol engine aeroplane packed with explosive and high octane fuel at night. When I was 19 my life revolved around girls, motorbikes, girls, cinema, rock and roll, and girls... well thinking about them. So I tried to write something of what I imagined my dad's life in his war years might have been.

The play is set on board "Lily" a Lancaster heavy bomber. The scenery when we presented it at the 2015 Hunstanton drama festival (and won first prize), was minimalistic. A forward facing chair for the nose gunner, two chairs raised on a small dais for the pilot and engineer, two chairs at a small table for the navigator and radio operator, a bar stool for the mid-upper gunner and a backward facing chair for the tail-end Charley. We used a lot of sound effects for the attacks, the engine noises and the crash, but for the guns we made the cast make "Dagga-dagga-dagga" noises. It could have been silly, but it wasn't.

There isn't a great deal of movement in the play, it relies more on the interaction between the crew. For the fighter attack everybody moved in unison, rolling and lurching in their respective chairs. For the death scene we had a single spot illuminating the rear gunner's position. Joe crawls past the pilot and engineer and lays slightly forward of the nose gunner for his bombing run. For the final crash we used a strobe to allow the cast to be tossed about like rag dolls, after the noise of a huge explosion and the brightest flash of light we could achieve.

I hope you enjoy presenting "L for Lily", and that you spare a thought for the real heroes of bomber command who fought for us in World War Two.

Steve Harper
2016

For my dad, Squadron Leader A.J. Harper DFC. Navigator and Bomb Aimer on the Lancaster "G" for George that flew in 635 Pathfinder squadron.

CHARACTERS

N.B Only volunteers were selected for flight crews, between 1939 and 1945; over 23,000 died. Their motto is "Per ardua ad astra"... Through adversity to the stars.

SKIP   Pilot Flight Lt

The captain. The only officer in the crew, a flight lieutenant since 1939. He joined the RAF in 1936 and has flown thirty missions in Sterlings and Wellingtons as the co-pilot. When his last squadron was re-deployed he found himself posted to Bexwell and given command of Lily, a brand new Lancaster bomber. He is the "old man" of the crew, and cannot believe how young the rest of the crew seem to be. The father figure, he maintains discipline but allows for a certain amount of youthful exuberance to keep morale up. He has flown ten missions with this crew, and has molded them into a capable fighting unit. His navigator Peter was recently married and requested a move to stay with his WAAF wife. Skip has selected Arthur as his replacement.

ERIC   Nose Gunner Sgt

Eric is a true cockney who comes from London's East End. His father is a docker and still can't believe Eric joined the RAF rather then follow him into the docks. Eric wanted the independence and a chance to fight for his country (although he would never admit to that). He is very self sufficient, and always the wheeler dealer (not always on the right side of the law). Can be a little short-tempered and used to settling most disputes with his fists; now however the RAF has given him self-discipline. After a brush with the magistrate that could have seen him being sent to Borstal, he volunteered for the RAF. A win-win situation that kept the magistrate happy, got Eric off with a warning and gave the RAF a first-class gunner.

NORMAN   Flight Engineer Sgt

Norman comes from Scunthorpe where his father runs a small garage. Always interested in mechanics he was doing evening classes at technical college when the war broke out. He volunteered straight away and was snapped up by the RAF to be trained as a flight engineer. Although he quite likes the WAAFs on the camp, his real passion is motorbikes. He is secretly extremely pleased that Skip selected him to train as the co-pilot, and has dreams where he heroically brings the plane in on one engine to the admiration of the group captain and the entire ground crew... Be careful what you wish for Norman.

JOE   Radio Engineer Sgt DFC

Joe worked for the BBC as a technician before the war. He also volunteered in 1939 and because of his background was trained by the Royal Core of Signals as a radio specialist. He requested a transfer to the RAF because of his interest in Radar (a new and secret method of seeing with radio waves). This makes him one of the more senior members of the crew. He gets on well with everybody and tends to look after the younger members. Joe is also on his second tour of duty having completed twenty-five missions in Wellingtons (bombers not boots), where he won the DFC. The group captain has recommended him for officer training.

ARTHUR   Navigator Sgt

The new boy. He was originally going to university but desperately wanted to do "his bit". As soon as he was old enough he volunteered and much to his mother's consternation joined the RAF. Always a studious mathematician he was a natural for navigation and got 92% in his passing out exam. He was immediately selected as a replacement for Lily's departing navigator and sent to Norfolk. Tonight will be his first real mission… Good luck Arthur. Although a competent navigator he is still very wet behind the ears when it comes to any other aspect of life as aircrew. He desperately wants to be accepted by the existing crew and to do well in his new job, but secretly is very frightened. (Just like everybody else.) He recently took Barbara, the cinema usherette out, and has saved his orange for her. (Again good luck with that.)

TAFF   Mid Upper Gunner Sgt

Merion Gwynth Williams is from the valleys of Wales. He is universally known as "Taff". He was suppose to go down the pits like the rest of his brothers. However, always a bit of a rebel, he volunteered for the RAF after a night drinking barley wine with Jones the milk. Considered by outsiders to be the clown of the crew, there is a side to Taff they do not see, a mature and caring man who not only keeps morale up, but also keeps a weather eye open for the others. You wouldn't want to fly without Taff at his guns… you really wouldn't.

TONY   Tail Gunner Sgt

Tony is the quiet and sensitive member of the crew. His "movie star" good looks bring him a lot of attention from the WAFFS on the camp, and a lot of envious ribbing from the other men. He keeps himself to himself, but visits a mysterious friend over near Bedford a lot. He does not talk about this. He is a popular member of the crew and does an excellent job as the "tail-end Charley". He sometimes joins the others on the sergeants' mess drinking nights, but usually declines invites to attending local dances. An impending court marshall weighs heavily on him. No-one else, even the skipper, knows of this.

The set comprises six chairs, a table and a stool arranged to make the seating on a Lancaster bomber. Two raised seats side by side for the pilot and engineer, **SKIP** *and* **NORMAN**. *A chair facing forward for the nose gunner,* **ERIC**. *A small desk with two seats for the navigator and radio operator,* **ARTHUR** *and* **JOE**. *A bar stool for the mid-upper gunner* **TAFF**, *and a single chair facing backwards for the "tail-end Charley"* **TONY**.

Lights up.

SKIP *stands on stage watching* **NORMAN** *who is banging parts of the set checking "Lily" is airworthy. The crew enters through the audience,* **ARTHUR** *is wearing a parachute. There is general banter as they make their way to the Lancaster.*

NORMAN *(indicating port inner engine)* There you are Skip, I asked the ground crew to change the gasket on the oil cooler and the leak has gone.

SKIP Jolly good Norman, *(noticing others)* Ah, there they are. Good grief is that young Arthur actually wearing his parachute to walk across the airfield?

NORMAN Hasn't taken it off since the briefing. He's new Skip, we all have to learn.

SKIP Yes I suppose you're right.

JOE Did you have the snook pie? It wasn't that bad tonight.

ERIC No mate, they had cod and chips down at the Crown.

ARTHUR But you must have paid for that.

ERIC Put it this way, you would have had to pay me to eat snook. I don't know what it is and I don't want to. Three and six for a nice bit of cod and a couple of pints of wallop seems a lot better to me.

They reach the plane.

SKIP Right everybody on board please. Time and the Groupie wait for no man. Arthur we don't usually wear our parachutes all the time. Give it to the armourers, and they will stow it away for you.

ARTHUR Yes sir, sorry sir.

ARTHUR *removes his parachute and everyone mounts the stairs and takes their place.*

TAFF I have never in all my born days known anybody as lucky as that jammy bastard.

ARTHUR Who's that Taff?

TAFF Oh yes very funny. That cockney tosser who took my last five bob, that's who. I mean my grandfather taught me to play crib. I've been playing since I was eight. But I never saw anybody get round a board like he does.

NORMAN This wouldn't be our exalted nose gunner the cockney all England Crib Champion, would it Taff?

TAFF Aye bloody Eric. Five bob. I was going to go to the pictures with that. *The Count of Monte Cristo* is on next week at the Majestic. I've got a date.

ERIC Well look on the bright side my old mucker. If you did manage to persuade a WAAF to go out with you, I'll win my other bet, and I'll bloody pay for you to get in.

TAFF Oh thanks mate. *(Pause)* Here hang on, what other bet?

JOE He's only winding you up. Anyway I'm going to go and see that, they reckon it's a cracking film. So who are you going to take then Taff?

TAFF Oh, well now, she's the business. Her name's Doris, and she works in the Opps Room. I was chatting her up in the NAAFI the other night. *(Conspiratorial)* Well I gazed into her eyes, and Doris my love I said, you could make a man very happy. And she said…

ALL BAAAAAAAA.

General laughter.

TAFF Oh yes very funny. *(Passing* **ARTHUR**'s *desk)* Oh that's nice Arthur. Silver isn't it?

ARTHUR Yes my propelling pencil. My mum and dad bought it for me. I do my calculations with it.

TAFF *(picking it up)* Worth a bob or two I should think.

ARTHUR Well…

JOE Hands off Taff, he isn't selling.

TAFF *(handing it back)* No, no, just saying it's nice though.

SKIP All right, all right, settle down please chaps. Radio check please.

All take seats.

JOE Aye Skip, you're patched through to the tower when you're ready. We're on 16.4 KCs for this op.

SKIP Thank you Joe… Bexwell Tower this is L for Lily, radio check on 16.4 KCs; how do you read me over? *(Pause)* Thank you Tower, we are green to go, repeat green to go, over. *(Pause)*

Roger that Tower, will wait for your signal. Over and out.

ARTHUR Do you think they will stand us down Skip?

SKIP Don't think so Arthur, the weather was clear over the target last Met report we got. We're up after O for Orange, keep an eye out for them Norman.

NORMAN Yes Skip.

ARTHUR But they might have technical reasons.

JOE Don't worry Arthur, this isn't too bad a run, we've done worse.

ERIC Yes bloody Happy Valley. Thank your lucky stars you were still training the last time we went there. It was rough so I reckon it's just tickety boo if we're not going there tonight.

TONY We lost U for Uncle and the Battleaxe in the flack.

NORMAN E for Echo went down in the channel on the way home.

TAFF And Z Zebra, got shot to hell by Junkers. Hard to see those buggers sometimes.

TONY You polish your Perspex like I told you Eric?

ERIC Well I got one of the ground crew to. Vinegar and brown paper, sounds like a bleedin nursery rhyme don't it?

TONY Yes but it works. No oil splashes or marks that you might think are fighters.

NORMAN Well if Tony recommends some sort of cleaning drill, I for one am for it. But I don't care if any of you fire at oil dribbles, just so long as you have enough ammo left to shoot at the real thing.

SKIP Amen to that. Keep it tight tonight chaps. This is our eleventh mission and I want to get back to my bacon and eggs in the mess tomorrow.

NORMAN Getting a wave from the ground crew Skip.

SKIP Starting engines.

> **SKIP** *opens a window and points at starboard inner engine, then rotates his finger. All members of the crew shake a little as the engine starts. Same procedure for the next three engines with the vibration increasing with each one.*

TAFF *(raising his voice)* Arthur's kept his orange skip.

> *Shaking and volume may now be reduced once* **SKIP** *closes the window.*

SKIP That will get your charts sticky Arthur.

ARTHUR I wont eat it on the flight Skip.

TAFF No, he's saving it for a girl when he gets back.

SKIP That's very generous of you Arthur, but flight crew get fresh fruit for a reason. It improves your night vision, or so the M.O. says. You eat it, and get your girl a choc ice.

ARTHUR *(embarrassed)* Yes Skip.

ERIC I don't know about an orange, but I'm dying for a fag.

TONY Oh, well you just go ahead and light up. I'm sure the explosives, high octane fuel, phosphorus and magnesium we're all crammed in with will be fine.

ERIC Yea, I know, I'm just saying I'm dying for a fag.

TONY Trouble is we don't want to die with you.

ARTHUR I've got some barley sugars if that will help Eric.

ERIC Oh thanks mate.

They crawl towards one another, and **ERIC** *takes a sweet.*

JOE Here mind my can Arthur.

ARTHUR What?

JOE My can, don't lose it.

ARTHUR What are you doing with an old tin can?

TAFF O give me strength.

ARTHUR What?

SKIP We all bring a can with us Arthur to take a leak in. You should know that.

ARTHUR Yes Skip, sorry Skip.

NORMAN You pee on my electrics, and you'll become part of the circuit.

TAFF Then that orange you saved won't do you any good at all.

JOE You share my can Arthur, OK?

TONY What did you do on your training flights Arthur?

ARTHUR Well, I just didn't want to go.

ERIC Yea right, only a couple of six-hour flights, you must have a bladder like a bull elephant mate.

TONY A full bladder and wind can cripple you at high altitude Arthur. Don't eat beans before a flight and always empty your bladder.

ARTHUR Right.

SKIP OK, lets just drop it shall we? There's a lot to pick up they didn't cover in training Arthur, but don't worry about it now. Oh hello, looks like we're moving.

TONY Not before time.

NORMAN O Orange is going Skip.

SKIP Right. Line me up Eric.

ERIC OK Skip… Right… Right… Left a touch Skip. Good.

SKIP How's that?

ERIC Spot on Skip, 180 on the nose.

SKIP Bexwell Tower this is L for Lily, we are set for take off…*(pause)* …Thank you Tower, keep a light in the window for us.

Right gentlemen, third star to the left and straight on till morning.

All begin to shake again, as **SKIP** *executes the take-off. Then stop as* **ERIC** *leads the singing to LILI MARLEEN. All crew lean back as the Lancaster takes off.*

ERIC *(sings)*

ALL *(except* **ARTHUR***)*

ALL *sway to the rhythm of the song and sing the first two verses of LILI MARLEEN, in German.*

TAFF You wasn't singing Arthur!

ARTHUR I don't speak German.

TAFF Terfuel ve only haf un Englander in ze crew.

ERIC Ve vil drop him out mit der cookie for Churchill. Und das vil teach him to be vun of ze master race, Ja.

JOE Zeig Heil.

SKIP All right, all right. Settle down chaps. First rendezvous point over Cromer please Arthur.

ARTHUR Yes Skip *(pause)* steer thirty-seven degrees magnetic. ETA fouteen minutes.

SKIP Thank you Arthur, perhaps we'll keep you along for the ride after all. Wheels up Norman?

NORMAN Check Skip wheels retracted.

ARTHUR Why were you singing in German?

TONY It can be a long old night if we don't have a bit of fun Arthur. You'll pick it up.

NORMAN So who was the lucky lady last night then Tony?

JOE Nobody on the camp I'll bet.

TAFF Yea, why don't you ever take one of the WAAFS out? I mean we've all tried it on with that Shirley; and been shot down. But come on Tony you're our secret weapon. I mean anybody who looks like a bleedin' movie star ought to take full advantage.

ERIC You're giving us Brylcreem boys a bad name Tony.

SKIP I think a fellow's got the right to choose his own lady friends Eric.

ERIC Well yea, but if you had his looks wouldn't you Skip?

SKIP I'm a married man. My philandering days are behind me.

NORMAN Only because you're ancient Skip.

JOE I think the pilot still has the right to order a crewman to bail without his chute Skip.

SKIP Thank you Joe I'll take that under consideration.

TONY Permission to test guns Skip.

SKIP Yes, everybody short bursts please. And Taff…?

TAFF Yes Skip.

SKIP Try not to shoot down one of ours.

TAFF O bloody hell Skip that was months ago.

ARTHUR What happened?

NORMAN About two months ago we had a Hurricane escort on a raid to Cologne.

JOE And when Taff tested his guns he got a bit close to a squadron leader in one of them.

TONY Shaved a bit off his tail.

ERIC He was a bit pissed off.

JOE I had to change the valves in my radio after he'd finished casting aspersions on Taff's parentage!

SKIP Yes well we won't let it happen again. I told you Taff either don't fire, or make a proper job of it so I don't have to do the paperwork.

TAFF Okey dokey Skip.

Pause.

SKIP The guns gentlemen.

TONY Aye Skip.

All three gunners make ah-ah-ah noises for two seconds.

Pause.

ARTHUR So do you have a young lady Tony?

TONY Nobody special Arthur, I just prefer not to get entangled with local girls, that can make it a bit messy.

TAFF I'd like to get a bit messy with that Shirley.

SKIP Yes thank you Taff, could we change the record please?

NORMAN Yes, so let me tell you about how I'm getting on with my little baby.

ERIC Our little baby Norman.

NORMAN Well yes, I suppose.

ERIC No suppose about it, I paid you the princely sum of six pounds so that I could have a ride on her when I needed to.

ARTHUR I say!

JOE No it's not what you think Arthur. Well go on Norman, tell Arthur about her.

NORMAN She's the most beautiful thing I've ever got my hands on. Some night it's just a pleasure to strip her down and grease her up.

ARTHUR I'm sorry I just don't like that sort of smut.

NORMAN No you barm pot. She's a 1.6 V twin Brough Superior motorbike with a twin cam KTOR JAP engine and a four-stud three-speed Sturmey Archer box. She'll do a hundred miles per hour. Or she will do once I've fitted my new rings to her.

ERIC Our new rings Norman.

NORMAN Yes all right Eric. I don't suppose you would like to help me one afternoon as it's our bike?

ERIC No chance. I'm the sleeping partner remember?

TONY Eric is financing the parts, Norman is doing the magic with the spanners and between them they hope to make a few bob hiring her out and winning a few road races.

ERIC And Tony is one of our regulars. He spends more time chasing crumpet over near Bedford then he does on the base.

TONY You get your money.

ERIC Oh yea, but I told you no more carving notches on the handlebars.

ARTHUR Gosh will it really do a hundred miles per hour?

NORMAN Yes, and if I can persuade the WO in charge of fitting, to let me have an old supercharger, I reckon I could squeeze a bit more out of her.

ARTHUR Sounds pretty dangerous.

JOE No more dangerous then popping over for a quick delivery to the old Fatherland.

TONY Yea, leave it out Joe, we don't need reminding.

JOE Sorry.

ARTHUR Six minutes to rendezvous point Skip, can we climb to fourteen thousand.

SKIP Yes, I'll take her up. Norman, what's going to happen when we go through the cloud?

NORMAN Er, temperature will drop Skip.

SKIP And?

NORMAN And the engines will run a bit rough until we adjust the mix.

SKIP Very good. What do we do then?

NORMAN We rebalance the engines because the oil will have become thicker.

SKIP Well done Norman we'll make a pilot of you yet. Right that's fourteen thousand. Get them back into sync for me.

NORMAN I'll try Skip.

Pause while **NORMAN** *handles the controls.*

SKIP No, not too rich, we want enough fuel to get back.

NORMAN Sorry Skip, how's that?

SKIP That's just about spot on. Thank you Norman.

ARTHUR Is Norman training for his wings?

JOE Not exactly.

TAFF We all learn each other's jobs Arthur, just in case.

ARTHUR Just in case of what?

TONY Just in case one of us gets wounded. Joe lets me play with the radio, Gee and ground display, it's all about getting us home. We've done ten raids together in Lily.

ERIC She's a lucky kite.

SKIP Well the crew skills help with the luck Eric, let's not forget that.

ARTHUR What happened to the last navigator Skip, did he...?

SKIP No, he just got transferred, on compassionate grounds.

TONY Peter married a WAAF, she got posted, so he put in a request to go with her.

JOE No thought for others, no offence Arthur but it's unlucky to change crew.

TONY Don't be stupid Joe, half the planes in the wing would be jinxed if that was true. Let's just be pleased we got somebody with Arthur's ability to guide us home. What percentage did you get in your nav tests Arthur?

ARTHUR Ninety two percent.

SKIP Right lets get this clear. Arthur was my choice to replace Pete, and I think we were lucky to get him. If we don't work as a team we are in trouble... OK?

Pause.

TAFF There's these two Scotsmen see.

JOE Oh here we go.

TAFF No this is a good one.

TONY Go on.

TAFF Yea, so there's these two Scotsmen... Angus and McTavish.

And Angus is on his deathbed.

SKIP Cheerful Taff.

TAFF Anyway, McTavish says to Angus *(bad Scots accent)* "Angus ma old friend, the doctor has just been, and he tells me that I'm dying."

TONY From the Punjab was he?

TAFF And Angus says, "Aye ma old friend I can see you're fading fast."

So McTavish props himself up on one elbow and he grasps Angus's arm.

NORMAN And gives him a kiss.

TAFF No, he says, "Angus, I want you to do something for me after I'm gone." "Och aye", says Angus, "and what will that be?"

"In the kitchen hidden in the meat safe, I've a bottle of twelve-year-old single malt," says McTavish.

SKIP Oh single malt, I remember that.

TAFF Yes, shut up Skip. "When I'm dead and laid to rest, I want you to pour it on to ma grave," says McTavish. "Will you do that for me Angus?"

ERIC What a waste.

TAFF Angus says, "Aye McTavish, you rest easy, I'll do that for you."

McTavish squeezes his hand and whispers, "Thank you old friend," as he slips away. Then still holding his old pal's hand Angus adds...

"You'll no mind if I strain it through my kidneys first though."

Laughter.

SKIP Right we are joining the main bomber stream. Everyone on the look out. We don't want to bump into any of the other crates. We're not insured for that.

JOE Got radio contact with F Foxtrot from C Flight Skip. They're at twelve-thousand feet on the same heading. It's Pete Barnes, you know the lad that won the darts last week.

NORMAN Can we climb a bit Skip, more height less flack remember?

SKIP Yes taking her up eighteen thousand feet, Norman?

NORMAN Trim set Skip.

JOE We try and get the old girl up to twenty thousand Arthur, less risk of fighters and flack.

ARTHUR How do we know there isn't another plane above us?

TONY See and be seen, but Stirlings can't make that altitude, and we're pretty spread out. The last wave will just be taking off now. So the odds are with us, and Joe keeps sweeping the frequencies for other contacts.

ARTHUR Three minutes to Dutch coast Skip.

SKIP Right everybody on maximum alert. We're in enemy airspace.

Give me a bearing for the target Arthur.

JOE Met report coming in, wind speed of fifteen knots at twenty thousand Arthur.

ARTHUR Er yes, OK er... Steer one hundred and twenty two degrees magnetic.

SKIP One hundred and twenty two it is, I'm going to try for a bit more altitude. Might get a bit bumpy, hang on to your dinners.

TONY What did you do before you joined up Arthur?

ARTHUR I was at university.

SKIP How long did you do before you volunteered Arthur?

ARTHUR Only the first two terms Skip.

JOE What was it you were studying?

ARTHUR Law.

TAFF There you are Eric, buy Arthur a few pints in the mess and he'll defend you at your next court-marshal.

ERIC Why don't you go and fu...

TONY FIGHTER. FIGHTER at two o'clock... Ah-ah-ah-ah-ah.

TAFF I'VE GOT HIM ah-ah-ah-ah-ah-ah.

NORMAN *(standing)* He's coming in low Skip.

SKIP Taking evasive action.

TONY Dive port Skip.

SKIP Corkscrewing, shout out where he is.

TAFF Coming round again twelve o'clock high.

TONY Ah-ah-ah-ah-ah.

TAFF Ah-ah-ah-ah-ah-ah.

SKIP Climbing starboard, where is he for Christ's sake?

ERIC I got him coming in head on Ah-ah-ah-ah-ah-ah.

TAFF Ah-ah-ah-ah-ah-ah.

TONY Ah-ah-ah-ah-ah... Smoke, he's hit, we got him. We got him.

NORMAN Anybody see him?

SKIP Climbing, for God's sake keep looking.

NORMAN I think he's gone Skip, we've lost him.

SKIP Right leveling out twenty thousand. Everyone OK, Tony?

TONY I'm OK Skip.

SKIP Taff?

TAFF Got a few new holes in the fuselage, but that's all. I'm claiming that as a kill.

SKIP Arthur, Joe?

JOE We've got a sixteen-inch hole just forward of the radio desk, but we're both OK Skip.

SKIP Eric?

ERIC Does cacking your pants count?

SKIP Not if you stay in your turret.

NORMAN Damage reports anybody?

Pause.

TAFF Getting a bit cold with the extra ventilation isn't it?

NORMAN Stuff some rag into it you daft Welsh sod. Now tell me Lily isn't a lucky kite, all engines ticking like a Swiss clock Skip.

TAFF *gets off of his stool and mimes packing out damage, before returning.*

ARTHUR Will we turn back now?

JOE No, the old girl's OK, none of us are hurt and we must be nearly there.

Pause.

ARTHUR Fifteen minutes to target.

JOE There you are then. If we turn back it doesn't count on our tally.

ARTHUR Right.

ERIC Look Arthur we're all scared, anybody who tells you different is lying, but we're a good crew, ten opps and not a scratch. So you just put that ninety two percent to work and we'll get home tickety boo.

ARTHUR Thanks Eric.

NORMAN I can see the green markers ahead Skip.

ARTHUR Course correction Skip, steer one hundred and twenty seven degrees. ETA to target twelve minutes.

JOE I'm picking up German fighter control Skip, they must have a few up tonight.

NORMAN Well bloody jam them then.

JOE All right, I'm just trying to get the exact frequency, don't want to tune into a harmonic.

SKIP Come on Joe.

JOE Got it, sending on their frequency Skip.

ERIC Hope that's blown their bloody eardrums out.

TONY I can see another Lanc, they're off to the west and about four thousand feet lower Skip.

SKIP Try and call them up Joe, I just want to make sure they know we are up here with them.

JOE Trying Skip.

ARTHUR Ten minutes to target Skip, you should see orange flares soon.

ERIC Orange flares dead ahead Skip.

TAFF Well done Arthur you got us to the party on time.

JOE Permission to go forward Skip.

SKIP Did you contact the other Lanc?

JOE Yes its V Victor from Debden Skip, they must be a bit off course, but they know we're here.

SKIP Right leave the jamming on and get in position.

JOE Aye Skip. *(Starts to crawl to front of plane to bomb aimers position)*

TONY Searchlights Skip, I can see lights to port.

ERIC Searchlights dead ahead as well Skip. Looks like they know we're on our way.

ARTHUR Oh bloody hell.

TAFF It's OK, eighteen thousand is about their limit.

TONY Oh shit, they've got that other Lanc in a beam, he's trying to dive out of it.

TAFF Jesus they just got him with another. Climb man, climb!

ERIC Flack's starting Skip, but they're all trying for V Victor.

TONY He's not corkscrewing, what the hell's the matter with them?

SKIP New pilot, he's forgotten all they taught him. Joe get back and try and call him up, tell him to roll port, climb and dive.

JOE *(turning round and starting to crawl back)* Yea, trying.

NORMAN Oh hell he's hit. He's lost half his bloody tail.

TONY He's rolling Skip, I can see flames.

TAFF It's both the port engines.

NORMAN *(standing)* Feather your props man, come on.

TONY He's hit again. He's going down Skip.

TAFF Jump you stupid sods, jump.

TONY I can see chutes Skip.

SKIP How many?

TONY Three, no four.

TAFF Come on, come on, get out.

TONY It's spinning too fast, nobody is going to get out now.

NORMAN Oh no!

ARTHUR What?

TAFF It just blew up, must have been carrying a cookie.

SKIP Chutes?

TONY Pretty sure all four were far enough away when she went Skip.

ARTHUR Are they dead?

SKIP Yes Arthur, three of them didn't make it. Now Joe get down the nose. Arthur ETA to target.

JOE On my way. *(He crawls to front of plane bomb aimer's position)*

ARTHUR They can't be dead, O God they can't be. It could be us next, they can't be, oh bloody hell, no, no.

SKIP Well they are sergeant, but we're not. Now give me time to target.

ARTHUR *(pause)* Yes sir, *(pause)* four minutes. Steer one hundred and twenty five should put you on the approach run. Sorry Skip.

SKIP Right. Norman, bomb doors open.

NORMAN Opening doors Skip. Hang on...

SKIP What?

NORMAN No it's OK, the port door seemed to stick, but it's down now.

JOE In position Skip. I can see the approach, go left a gnats.

SKIP One degree port.

JOE Right that's it. Hold it steady Skip.

ERIC Flack's starting, could get bumpy.

NORMAN All controls are green Skip.

ARTHUR Three minutes.

JOE I've got red markers Skip.

SKIP Right, I'm handing control over. You're flying the plane Joe.

JOE Right fuses on, bomb sight on, selector on salvo. I can just make out the Elbe. Moonlight's reflecting off it.

ARTHUR Come on, come on.

TAFF This is the worse bit. How long?

ARTHUR Two minutes.

> *Large bang of exploding flack.*

JOE Steady, steady. Yellow markers. Shit that was close.

NORMAN Losing oil pressure in port outer.

ARTHUR We must be there Joe, just drop them.

JOE Wait...wait... Left a little Skip.

SKIP Left a touch, how's that Joe?

TAFF Oh for Christ's sake...

JOE Steady, steady... I can see it, nearly, nearly...wait...wait...

ERIC Come on mate the flack's getting worse.

NORMAN *(prays sotto voice)*, Holy Mary mother of God, pray for us sinners, now and at the hour of our, of our death.

ARTHUR Please Joe, just drop them. Oh Jesus.

JOE Hold her steady Skip. Got the target in my bomb sight, steady, steady...wait...now... Bomb's gone.

Everybody lurches as the plane jumps with lost weight.

SKIP Right let's say ten seconds for the photo flash...*(long pause)*... and evasive action, climbing, how's the port outer Norman?

Another louder bang **TAFF**, **ARTHUR** *and* **NORMAN** *are thrown out of their seats.* **TONY** *slumps forward.* **SKIP** *grabs his left arm.*

Aghhh I'm hit, I'm hit. I can't hold her.

NORMAN *(climbing back)* All right Skip, hang on... Joe get up here, Skip's hurt.

JOE Coming. *(Climbs into cockpit area with first aid kit)* Let's see Skip.

SKIP It's my arm, think it's broken.

JOE *(examining him)* You're OK, you're OK Skip, it's shrapnel. It's gone through, but it's busted your radius. Not bleeding too bad. Hang on, I'll give you some morphine.

Injects **SKIP** *in leg.*

SKIP Shit! Shit! Shit! That hurts.

NORMAN Hold on Skip the morphine will cut in soon.

JOE How is it?

SKIP Oh yes, that's better, bloody hell that's better. Think I'll just shut my eyes…

JOE He's passed out. Right I'm going to bandage his arm and splint it up. Skip, Skip, can you hear me? No he's out of it. You all right to chauffeur us home Norm? (*JOE gets* SKIP *out of his seat and lays him on the floor. He then bandages* SKIP*'s arm and puts a sling on it/* NORMAN *reluctantly takes the pilot's seat.*)

NORMAN Oh Christ, wake him up Joe, I can't fly this thing on my own, I'm the engineer not the flaming pilot. Come on Joe give him something, it's only a broken arm. I'll be OK if he tells me what to do.

ARTHUR What's happening!

JOE Skip's busted his arm, Norman's taking us home.

NORMAN I can't I tell you, there's too much to flying this, it's a four-engine heavy bomber not a bloody bi-plane.

ERIC Right listen up Norman. Dead is bad. Anything not dead is better. We are still flying, but we need to get the hell out of here before some sodding Messerschmitt finds us. Now if Lily was a bleeding motorbike you wouldn't think twice about fettling her or whatever you northern types do with machinery. How hard can it be you feed the engines petrol, you turn the control stick towards Blighty and you put your bleedin' foot down, savvy?

NORMAN But it's not as simple as that…

ERIC I don't care. Just fly the bloody thing to a bit of English sky before you start whinging.

ARTHUR Come on Norman mate, you can do it; piece of cake.

TAFF I don't want to state the obvious see, but you're the only one who the Skip trained. That means our best chance of getting home is you being the pilot. Come on boyo, tell us what we can do to help.

NORMAN Oh shit, shit, shit…(*pause*) Right Arthur I need a course for the Dutch coast.

ARTHUR Already done Norm, steer two hundred and sixty magnetic.

NORMAN Two hundred and sixty. Hang on everybody I'm going to try to get more height. Oh Christ the controls don't feel right.

JOE You're doing all right Norm, she's turning, port outer sounds a bit rough though.

NORMAN Right richer mix, I'm going to give her a bit of flap to help the turn, I've seen the Skip do that.

ERIC See, not as hard as you thought. Just like a bike.

NORMAN Yes, piece of cake. Next time I get the bike up to eighteen thousand feet I'll get you to ride pillion.

TAFF You're doing OK.

ARTHUR That's two hundred and sixty Norman. Just fly her straight and level and we'll get home.

JOE Well done mate, the Skip would be proud of you. Shouldn't we check everyone else is OK now?

NORMAN Yea, just let me level her out. I'll need you to keep an eye on the heading Arthur. Eric, you OK?

ERIC Yea, I am now mate it looks like Dante's bloody inferno down there.

NORMAN Taff?

TAFF Yea, I'm fine.

ARTHUR Steer two degrees west Norman.

NORMAN Right. Tony. *(Pause)* Tony, call in will you? *(Pause)* Shit. Taff get down there his radio line might just have failed.

TAFF On my way. *(Crawls to rear gunner position)* Oh no, no.

He opens **TONY**'s *flying jacket to reveal a big pile of red ribbon.*

(shouts) Joe get up here with the medical kit, quick as you like. *(He cradles* **TONY** *in his arms)*

JOE Coming Taff.

JOE *picks up medical satchel and crawls to rear of plane.*

TAFF Tony, can you hear me? Listen mate we'll have you fixed up in no time, just hang on for me OK?

TONY *(whisper)* Hurts.

TAFF I know mate, just hang on. Joe where are you?

JOE *(arrives)* Here. Give him two of these first.

Hands over morphine ampoules which **TAFF** *injects into* **TONY***'s leg.*

TAFF There you go Tony mate, just give it a minute.

TONY Ahhhh. *(Drums heels on floor)* Oh Jesus, how bad is it Taff?

TAFF Well I reckon that's your last opp for at least a month.

TONY Don't bullshit me Taff, how bad?

TAFF *(pause)* Bad.

JOE Let me try and get a compression bandage on it.

> **TAFF** *opens* **TONY***'s jacket to reveal ribbons. He and* **JOE** *exchange glances.*

TAFF I'd just let him lay quiet like for a bit.

TONY Bit of a bugger really. I had a lot to sort out.

JOE Plenty of time for that mate. As soon as we land we'll have an ambulance waiting.

TONY Too late Joe. I'm cold, really cold.

TAFF No you'll be fine.

TONY I want you to do something for me.

JOE You'll be OK mate.

TAFF What do you want Tony?

TONY Want you to go and see somebody.

JOE Who is it.

TONY His name's Alan, Alan Turing. He's one of the boffins at a place called Bletchley Park. Tell him I'm sorry, and I died thinking of him.

JOE I don't understand Tony, what are you saying?

TAFF Go and keep an eye on my guns Joe, we're a sitting duck with two turrets out.

JOE But–

TAFF Just do it.

JOE OK Taff, you be OK with Tony. There's more morphine in the satchel.

TAFF We'll be fine. Just yell if you see anything.

JOE goes back to the mid turret.

What are you sorry about?

TONY Sorry I ruined his career. Sorry we can't be together. Sorry I'll never see him again. He'll know.

TAFF I'll tell him. Does anybody else know?

TONY Yes, we got caught Taff. It's hit the fan big time.

TAFF Don't worry. *(pause)...* Does he love you?

TONY Yes.

TAFF Then to hell with all of them.

TONY But it's his career Taff, he's so clever. He's doing so much, and I spoiled it all, just because I wanted to be with him. I was going to be court-marshaled. We broke the law by falling in love.

TAFF It will be fine. Just lay quiet and... Tony... Tony... Oh

Christ NO!

*He embraces **TONY** then lays him gently on the floor. He weeps, before crawling forward to **JOE**.*

Oh bloody, bloody hell Joe.

JOE Is he?

TAFF Aye, the morphine worked and he wasn't in any pain at the end, but he's gone. I'm sorry.

JOE What was all that about saying sorry to some chap at Bletchley?

TAFF *(pause)* Oh some girl's father. You know.

JOE Good old Tony hey Taff.

TAFF Yea, good old Tony. Right I'll take over, you better get back and tell the others. You OK with that?

JOE Yea, I just can't believe he's dead.

> JOE *turns and crawls back to the desk.* TAFF *sits on the barstool.*

NORMAN How is he?

JOE *(shakes his head)* He's gone mate, he just slipped away.

ERIC Never!

JOE Shrapnel made a mess of him. I'm sorry.

ARTHUR What, Tony's dead?

JOE He wasn't in any pain at the end. He was talking about some girl he wanted Taff to go and say sorry to her father.

ERIC I bet he broke a few hearts in his time.

NORMAN A bit of a legend our Tony.

ARTHUR Oh bloody hell.

SKIP Uhhh, blood and sand, what's happening?

ERIC It's the morphine Skip. Bit like having one over the eight I reckon.

SKIP Morphine... Oh yes, but my arm's stopped feeling like it's got a number fifteen bus parked on it. Right Norman my boy how are you doing?

NORMAN Err, yes, piece of cake Skip, but we've lost Tony. Flack.

SKIP Oh no, Jesus no. Everybody else OK?

TAFF We're fine Skip, I'm covering the rear.

SKIP Thanks Taff, yell if you need help.

ERIC Tell you what Skip, old Norm here's a natural. He just took over and got us out of the drop zone, cool as a cucumber. He deserves a medal.

SKIP Yes I think he might. All right Norm if you're going to get a gong you better get us home. You will be hands-on in every sense of the word.

NORMAN I don't think the port outer is going to hold out Skip. I'm going to turn it off. The oil pressure is all to hell.

SKIP I agree, shut the fuel cock and feather the prop. *(Pause)* She still seems to be yawing to port. Have you shut the bomb doors?

NORMAN Damn!

SKIP You can't remember everything. Shut them now.

Pause.

NORMAN They won't close Skip, they're jammed.

ARTHUR Shall I go and see?

NORMAN Yes, but be careful. We don't want you falling out.

ARTHUR Won't be long. *(Crawls off to bomb bay)*

ERIC You want to go with him Joe, that's a long way down.

JOE *(pause)* No, he's coming back.

ARTHUR There's a bomb jammed in the door mechanism, I can't move it.

SKIP What sort of bomb?

ARTHUR It's about a yard long, green with two bright red stripes.

NORMAN and **ERIC** Thirty-pound incendiary.

SKIP Is the nipple at the front all right?

ARTHUR Don't know Skip.

SKIP Get back and check, take Joe with you.

ARTHUR Right. Why?

SKIP Because that's what arms the bomb. If it gets pushed in, it fires the primer.

ARTHUR and JOE crawl to bomb bay. JOE holds ARTHUR's belt while he leans forward to inspect bomb.

JOE Can you see the nose?

ARTHUR Yes, it's still attached to the broken release mechanism, it's bumping against the fuselage Joe.

JOE Norman can you hear, it's a thirty pounder with a self setter?

NORMAN Try and stop the nose hitting anything that's what triggers the fuse.

JOE Arthur, try and get the nose away from the plane.

ARTHUR *(leaning even further forward)* I can't reach it.

JOE Did you hear he can't reach it?

NORMAN There's a small hole about eighteen inches back from the nose, about a quarter-inch. Very carefully jam something in there. But for Christ's sake do it carefully. There's thirty pounds of phosphorus and high explosive in that thing.

ARTHUR What did he say?

JOE Have you got anything metal on you? About a quarter-inch wide.

ARTHUR Er, I've got my silver propelling pencil.

JOE Perfect.

ARTHUR My parents bought it for me.

JOE Arthur, I want you to very, very carefully take your lovely pencil and ease it into a little hole Norman says will be eighteen inches back from the nose. Can you see that?

ARTHUR *(pause)* Yes, I think so.

JOE Can you reach it?

ARTHUR Ughhhh yes.

JOE Push the pencil in.

ARTHUR It's too tight.

JOE Push harder Arthur.

ARTHUR It will scratch it.

JOE ARTHUR!

ARTHUR All right, but it was nearly new. Ughhh. *(Pause)* Yes, it's in.

JOE Is it secure?

ARTHUR Errr yes, I think so.

JOE Good boy. Norman, did you hear? He's done it.

SKIP Is it tight? Because if it falls out we could all miss breakfast.

ARTHUR As tight as I could get it Skip. It was scratched.

ERIC Bloody hell Arthur we'll get you a twenty-four carat gold 'un.

SKIP Right get back up here.

> **JOE** *and* **ARTHUR** *return to flight deck.*

NORMAN I need a course, and Joe we need an ambulance waiting.

JOE I'm on it.

ARTHUR Steer two hundred and ninety seven the wind's getting stronger. The Dutch coast is twelve minutes. Can you watch out for me Eric?

ERIC I'll yell as soon as I see it.

JOE I'll give you another shot of morphine Skip.

SKIP No, I'll yell when I need one, I think I need a clear head to give Norman as much help as I can.

TAFF Can I do anything to help?

SKIP Just keep alert Taff, we aren't out of the woods yet. You have to cover the rear of Lily as well.

TAFF OK, you all right flying on three engines with the bomb doors open Norman?

NORMAN Losing power on starboard outer Skip.

SKIP Let me look, temperature one hundred and four, pressure fifty five, it must have broken some valves. Can you turn off the fuel cock Norman? We can't have far to go. We'll fly home on the inners, slower, but it should be easier to hold.

NORMAN Losing altitude Skip.

SKIP Right, make the mix richer and open the throttles to one thousand four hundred revs.

NORMAN We don't have that much fuel left.

SKIP Arthur what's the nearest airfield to us when we cross the channel?

ARTHUR Well it's either Sculthorpe or West Raynham. But we'd be in spitting distance of Bexwell with either of those. Steer three hundred and twenty Norman, I'll correct you for whichever you choose.

SKIP Let's try and get Lily back. I'd like to get Tony home as well. Steer three hundred and twenty magnetic, ease up on the throttles Norman, and bring her down to five thousand feet. You're doing all right old son.

ERIC I can see Blighty, boys, we're going to make it.

TAFF That's a wonderful bloody sight even if it isn't Wales.

NORMAN How far Arthur?

ARTHUR About seventy miles…that's eight minutes.

SKIP Radio in and tell them about Tony, and that Norman's bringing us in. I want the main runway clear, and I want an ambulance on standby.

JOE *(pause)* Done that Skip, they advise runway two, as less cross winds.

SKIP Two it is, heading please Arthur.

ARTHUR One hundred and fifty eight degrees Skip, recommend we lose altitude.

SKIP Bring her round to one hundred and fifty eight, that's good Norman, now throttle back and three quarter flap. That's it. Right wheels down. Piece of cake hey?

NORMAN Yes like I said Skip. Just not as easy as it looks.

Pause.

ERIC Skip, can you see the port wheel from there?

SKIP No.

ERIC It's flat.

TAFF You sure?

ERIC Pretty much. Must have taken a hit.

ARTHUR What do we do?

SKIP Does it look as though it's still on the rim Eric?

ERIC Yes, just flat.

SKIP We've got three choices Norman. Retract the wheels and try a belly landing. Or bring her in on the flat.

ARTHUR So what's the third choice?

NORMAN We get Lily as high as we can and you jump.

TAFF Why can't we all jump?

SKIP Because we've still got that bomb on board, and not enough fuel to get her over the channel.

NORMAN I'd rather try with the wheels down Skip.

SKIP Me too.

TAFF Well I for one am not jumping, never did like the idea of stepping out into nothing.

ERIC Yea, count me in, I'm staying.

JOE You're going to need an extra pair of hands to haul her back Norman.

ARTHUR And I'm part of L for Lily's crew.

SKIP Right line her up Norman, here we go.

NORMAN Full flaps.

SKIP Revs down to one hundred and eighty.

NORMAN Throttling back.

ERIC Here it comes.

TAFF Oh Jesus H Christ.

JOE We're skewing, more rudder Norman.

ARTHUR We're too fast.

SKIP Get ready to hold her on the yolk when we touch down, she's going to pull to port with everything she's got.

NORMAN Braking aghhhhhh.

JOE Aghhhhhh.

SKIP Straighten her, straighten her, we're going off the runway.

NORMAN Can't hold her.

ERIC Brake we're nearly there. Come on Norm... Yes, yes, yes.

SKIP We've done it, we're down, Norman we're down. Cut engines, fuel off. We've done it, well bloody hell.

Long pause.

ARTHUR Is it always like this?

TAFF *(appearing from mid turret)* No it bloody isn't. Oh here you are Arthur, found this on the bomb bay floor. It's your silver pencil thing. Lucky hey, it could have fallen out.

ARTHUR But what's stopping the bomb now?

NORMAN Oh God, nooooooo.

Sound and light effects of massive explosion. A strobe light will allow the cast to be thrown down on the stage where they lay like rag dolls. Followed by:

Blackout.

And sound effect of Marlene Dietrich singing LILI MARLEEN that fades to silence.

END

Property List

It is set aboard a 1943 Lancaster bomber, which will be depicted with a minimal set comprising of only chairs, and tables.

Sound Effects

Music from 633 squadron.
Lancaster engines,
Fighter aircraft with machine guns.
Explosion 1 (flack)
Explosion 2 (louder flack)
Explosion 3 (bomb detonating)
Marlene Dietrich singing *LILI MARLEEN*.

Lighting

Searchlights sweep the sky (I had intended to have two people sitting either end of the front row with powerful torches)

Death scene (I would like only the rear gunner lit, with the rest of the plane in very low lighting.

Final explosion

Lightning Source UK Ltd.
Milton Keynes UK
UKOW04f0933110816

280406UK00001B/8/P